Christian Acts of Kindness

The Random Acts of Kindness™ Foundation

Foreword by Millard D. Fuller

Founder, Habitat for Humanity International

Grace House

Walnut Creek, California

Grace House books are distributed by Publishers Group West.

Cover illustration and calligraphy: Brenda Walton

Cover design: Ame Beanland

Library of Congress Cataloging-in-Publication Data

Christian acts of kindness / the Random Acts of Kindness Foundation : foreword by Millard Fuller.

ISBN: 1–57324–173–3 (pbk).

1. Kindness—Religious aspects—Christianity Anecdotes.

I. Random Acts of Kindness Foundation.

BV4647.K5C48 1999 99–23771

241'.677—dc21 CIP

Printed in the United States of America on recycled paper

99 00 01 02 03 DATA 10 9 8 7 6 5 4 3 2 1

Hurting, they came to Him,
Healed, they followed Him.
Grateful, they gave to Him what they had and what they were.
Blessed, they became a blessing
and went out to all the world in His name.

Those who are hurt
and healed
grateful
and blessed
still move among us
in His name.

—Ann Weems

Foreword

by Millard D. Fuller

Some people believe that random kindness is ineffectual and naive. They believe that if you want to change the world, if you want to alleviate suffering, hunger, joblessness, or homelessness, you need to be pointed and intentional and specific and planned in your kindness. They argue that to create an opportunity for effectual change in either individuals or society as a whole, you need to be not only creative in your kindness, but also strategic.

They have a point. Wisdom doesn't leave the room when Compassion walks in. I would never argue (and I doubt you would either) that analysis, strategy, and evaluation are the enemies of kindness. In many cases they are absolutely crucial.

The problems of our age are complex, and they require complex, careful, strategic responses. The problems of poverty, hunger, homelessness, famine, and disease will not be solved by goodwill alone.

In fact, if you look at the organization I work for, Habitat for Humanity, you'll see a very deliberate, methodical approach to eliminating poverty housing around the world. At Habitat for Humanity, we don't just throw our money (or our houses) at people who need them. Instead, we create partnerships with families in need, and offer them not a hand out, but a hand up, out of poverty. At Habitat, we believe strongly that people should live in dignity and grace, and in nearly all cases that takes long, hard, careful planning. Hardly random acts.

And yet, I believe—absolutely and unwaveringly—in the power and necessity of random kindness. In fact, I'd go so far to say that unplanned, nearly accidental encounters in which people offer one another unexpected and undeserved kindness are at the bedrock of our Christian witness.

Why? Because it is in random, unplanned, unselfish, reckless kindness that we get the best picture of the nature of the grace God gave us in Christ. You see, no matter how effectual our methodical, careful kindnesses may be, they still look something like the law. We plan and strategize so that our actions make the most difference for the most deserving, and when it's all said and done, we hope to be fair. But fairness has little to do with the Christian gospel. In fact, if the gospel were fair, we would be (as Saint Paul suggested of life without the Resurrection) the "most miserable" of people.

At the heart of the Good News that Christ proclaimed is the notion that the most undeserving, difficult, and doggedly frustrating persons among us are the very ones that Christ came to be with, to love, and to save. "While we were yet sinners," the Scripture proclaims, "Christ died for us." He didn't wait until we met Him partway, became somehow less a sinner, or until we fit into His strategic plan. He just loved us, in His way, out of His way, along the way.

Jesus had a plan, to be sure. But His plan was designed to embrace those tremendous, extraordinary split-seconds of opportunity for which no planning can be adequate, for which the only good and gracious response is to put aside the plan and embrace the moment, and do whatever kindness demands. "Suffer the children to come to me, and forbid them not."

Jesus was surrounded by strategists and forward planners who were constantly longing for the new order of the Kingdom of God. Jesus, however, understood that the Kingdom was and is here, right now, in those moments of unexpected mercy, unrehearsed tenderness, unmerited grace. Jesus understood that it is in those moments when we are on the edge of recklessness, when we are stretched beyond our abilities to heal and our capacity to be kind, and yet still extend a hand in kindness, that we tumble into the place where we are empowered to do "beyond all that we could ask or think." It was into those moments that He led his disciples, and it is still into those places that He calls us now. Random acts of kindness? I say Yes! You should, too.

The Challenge of Compassion

Two thousand years ago, the most remarkable event in human history took place: Because of love, divine compassion, and kindness, God became human. We cannot, in our limited human existence, begin to understand the breadth and scope of that single act of love. Nor can we truly understand what it is about our feeble construction of flesh and blood that makes us worthy of such love. However, we can at the very least be guided by this extraordinary sacrifice. When Christ walked this earth, His footsteps laid out the path for us to follow; it is not a path of burdensome obligation or duty, it is the example of the single most selfless act of love and kindness.

Applying this most simple yet extraordinary message to our own lives, however, seems at times challenging beyond our capacity to respond. The tumbling growth and expansion of human endeavor dazzles and amazes us. It is easy to get distracted and lose our focus. Especially now, at the turning of the millennium, we are flooded with information, opportunities, and options. In trying to get through daily life as we know it, we tend to forget that we are here for a larger purpose, and that that purpose encompasses everyone and everything in creation. It is easy to see only what is in front of us, to care for only what is close, to love only those who agree with us. But just as Christ never put limits on His love, so must we constantly remind ourselves that we were created for so much more than just getting by.

At times, when we notice the astonishing beauty of the world we inhabit, when, as if out of the corner of our eye, we glimpse the awesome majesty of this creation, we are lifted up and returned back to the essential nature of our souls. But then again, when we are confronted by the destructiveness we are capable of and the human depths of depravity we are responsible for, we feel overwhelmed and find it difficult to hold the simplest truths close to our hearts. However, we have no alternative; we are the purpose and the product of Christ's sacrifice. Our lives, through Christ's love, were imbued with meaning long before any of us who are alive today existed, and we are being called now to wake up, to pay attention, to live our lives through His example.

What was set in motion so long ago is now in our hands. We received the most precious of all gifts—the lesson of sacred love and divine kindness—and it is now up to us either to ignore that gift or to learn how to live our lives in a way that reflects and honors our sacred role. To truly be a Christian means to act in the world as Christ would have acted. It means that we need to overcome our human frailties, rise above our petty concerns, and open our hearts to the very roots of our lives. It is a daunting task, one that we feel ill-equipped to perform in our current state. However, through Christ's example we have received the simplest and most exquisite guide to living a meaningful life: Treat everyone, even the most debased sinner, with love and kindness. If we follow that simple path—love and kindness—we can never go wrong.

If somehow in our struggle to be faithful, in our earnest devotion, in our desire to hew to the narrow path laid out for us we lose track of this most simple message, then we must know that we have lost our way. Love, compassion, and kindness are Christ's beacons guiding us forward. We need never to let those tools slip from our hands, and we need to remember that these soft, beautiful words—*love, compassion,* and *kindness*—are divine instruments of extraordinary power.

When most people think of power, they think of things like brute physical strength, political might, military power, or the power of the wealthy to buy whatever they want. But these forms of power are illusory. Certainly they exist, and yes, they can push and pull and appear to have an immediate and dramatic impact, but that impact begins to fade immediately. Real power unfolds softly, winds into the very fiber of our souls, and then grows stronger each day. It is the capacity to alter someone's life for the better with just a smile or a helping hand. Real power rises out of all the acts of kindness and compassion we bring into the world and connects us more deeply to each other and to our divine purpose.

It is sometimes difficult to believe this, but those of us alive today have been gifted. We see a world that is overwhelming in size and scope, that appears to us to be bursting at its seams with massive and intractable problems. We seem incapable of fulfilling what should be our most fundamental responsibilities of feeding the hungry and clothing and providing shelter for the poor. All this is painfully true; but so too is the fact that for the first time in history we have both the resources and the skills to solve these problems. The only issue is whether we have the faith to succeed. We live at a special time; we have been honored and charged with the task of bringing humanity into its full potential, but it is a task that can only be accomplished if we can somehow remember and incorporate the deepest lessons from Christ's life into our own existence. We have come full circle from Christ's living example through 2,000 years of exciting and escalating human development to today's choice before us. We will either remake our world into a place that radiates love and kindness, or we will perish in an Armageddon of our own making. The choices are so clear, the challenge seems overwhelming; but we have our beacons—love, kindness, and compassion—and if we can keep them evermost in our hearts and minds, we will succeed.

Brotherly love is still the distinguishing badge of every true Christian.

—*Matthew Henry*

I grew up with seven brothers and sisters on a small ranch in Montana. It was a hard life, but for a while we got by OK with my father working a second job in town. But then times got tough and my father lost his job. I was fifteen years old when it became clear we weren't going to be able to continue. After a few months of reading the classified ads I found a job in Portland, Oregon.

My parents scraped up enough money to get me there with the hope that I would be able to send a little money home now and then. When I got to Portland, I found out that the store I was supposed to be working at had just gone out of business. I guess in the midst of their own troubles they had forgotten to let me know.

Stuck in Portland with less than a dollar in my pocket, I had no idea what to do, so I started walking back to Montana. I had gotten about five miles out of town when an elderly couple heading home to their farm from church stopped to ask me what I was doing out on this road all alone. When I told them, they invited me to stay at their farm for a while to see if anything would turn up. I lived there, helping out where I could. Every Sunday we would travel into town for church and they would introduce me to as many people as possible, making sure to let everyone know I was in need of a job.

Sure enough, six weeks later I got hired by one of the people they had introduced me to, and I've lived happily in Portland ever since. I'm now ninety-three years old, and though it was seventy-eight years ago when that wonderful couple took me home with them, not a day of my life has gone by without my remembering what they did for me.

Happiness comes from spiritual wealth, not material wealth. . . . Happiness comes from giving, not getting. If we try hard to bring happiness to others, we cannot stop it from coming to us also. To get joy, we must give it, and to keep joy we must scatter it.

—*John Templeton*

I have spent all of my adult life working with the very poor and homeless as a Christian lay minister, and I have been filled over and over by those I serve. I've gone full circle on giving a few times. I started out by literally giving the shirt off my back and then some, and began to think that "they" wouldn't benefit from this, that "they" might abuse the money, or heaven forbid, even me. Then I took some time out to think about what Jesus would do and realized how simple He made it. He gave us the most perfect blueprint possible. He said, when asked, "Give!" We don't have to assess a situation, figure out whether it is the real thing or not, worry about abuses or rip-offs. All we have to do is give. Pretty simple, eh?

I am only one; but still I am one. I cannot do everything, but still I can do something. I will not refuse to do the something I can do.

—Helen Keller

One cold Friday night, the youth group at our church wanted to go into the neighborhood and show God's love in a practical way. So we got out the shovels and proceeded to walk around asking our neighbors if they would like us to shovel their driveways. Some were hesitant, but others were happy to receive our gesture. We came to one house where no one was home. The driveway desperately needed to be cleared, so we just proceeded to shovel away.

While we were there, the lady of the house returned. I thought it might be a little uncomfortable for her to find five youths she didn't know in her driveway, so I explained what was going on. She was overjoyed. It turned out that her husband was out of town and she had been working long hours.

She went into the house and came back out a few minutes later to tell us that she had just called her husband to let him know there were angels in her driveway. She was blessed. So were we. The true love of God is as easy to share as shoveling snow from a driveway.

She stretches out her hand to the poor; yea, she reaches forth her hands to the needy.

—*Proverbs 31:20*

I've always thought of myself as a devoted believer, but this last year I have learned something important about my faith. There was a homeless woman who used to hang around on the street I walked down on my way to the market; to be honest, she always made me very nervous. It wasn't just that she was dirty, but it seemed to me that she was looking at me in an odd way every time I walked by. I would hurry my steps and keep my eyes glued to the pavement as I went past. But as time went by I began to feel ashamed of my behavior. When I really looked into my heart I knew I was treating her as if she didn't exist, whereas if I really wanted to live what I told myself I believed in, I should at the very least treat her with the same respect that any of us deserves.

One evening as I was wrapping up leftovers from dinner, I decided on an impulse to take a warm plate down the street to see if the woman was there. When I saw her she was already staring at me; my heart started to race, but I forced myself to look her in the eyes as I walked over to sit by her and offer her the dinner. She gave me a huge smile, thanked me, and praised my cooking to the sky. While she ate we talked a little, and to my own surprise I found myself asking her why she stared at me so much.

She said, "I'm sorry, honey, I didn't mean to upset you," and then jumped up to fish a photograph out of the big plastic bag she always carried with her. The photo was pretty crumpled, but the image was clear as day and looked like it could have been a twin sister I never had. She pointed at the picture and said, "That's my sister Claire, she died ten years ago and I miss her something terrible. I don't mean to stare, but you look so much like her it lets me imagine her alive for a few minutes."

What we give to the poor. . . is what we carry with us when we die.

—*Peter Marin*

Once or twice a year my family and I (I'm in seventh grade) go to Glide Memorial Church in San Francisco. It's a church where every day volunteers help to feed the homeless. And on special times of the year like Christmas and Thanksgiving they have a big blowout. Anyway, a couple of times a year I volunteer to help serve food and pass out eating utensils. One year a special little girl no older than ten gave me flowers. Till this day, I still have the flowers. I will always remember that girl.

Kindness is the dove of God
Who overshadows the darkness,
As it glides along the earth with its silver wings.
Its golden eyes seek and destroy the darkness
And restore peace to the land.

—*Jim Tran, age ten*

My brother was a P-47 pilot in World War II. He was shot down over Germany in 1945, and we became an MIA family for four years. For years, our government searched Europe for graves and/or the remains of missing servicemen. In 1949, my brother's grave was found. In an unbelievable act of kindness (in wartime no less), someone had buried him with his ID tags.

As a family, we elected to bury him with his buddies in the American Military Cemetery near Liege, Belgium, with over 5,000 other American servicemen. We have visited that cemetery on several occasions, but this day was the fiftieth anniversary service at the cemetery, and my husband and I were there.

After the ceremonies of great dignity and greater emotions, we walked to the section where Jimmy is buried. Hundreds of people were quietly passing among the graves. As I wept beside my brother's grave, a Belgian woman came up to me, kissed both my cheeks, and held me close. She thanked me for the sacrifice our family made for her country. She then said, "I realize you can't come here often. I belong to a group of Belgian citizens who come here once a month to offer prayers at random graves. May I adopt your brother? I will be here monthly to pray for him and for you."

We were both weeping. Almost as quietly as she appeared, she was lost in the crowd. I never saw her again or learned her name.

Give, and it will be given to you: good measure, pressed down, shaken together, and running over will be put into your bosom. For with the same measure that you use, it will be measured back to you.

—*Luke 6:38*

It was only four days before Christmas. The spirit of the season hadn't yet caught up with me, even though cars packed the parking lot of our local discount store. Inside the store, it was worse. Shopping carts and last-minute shoppers jammed the aisles. "Why did I come today?" I wondered. My feet ached almost as much as my head. My list contained names of several people who claimed they wanted nothing, but I knew their feelings would be hurt if I didn't get them something. Trying to come up with gift ideas for people who had everything, and deploring the high cost of goods, I considered gift buying anything but fun.

Hurriedly, I filled my shopping cart with items and proceeded to the long checkout lines. In front of me were two small children—a boy of about five and a younger girl. The boy wore a ragged coat. Enormously large, tattered tennis shoes jutted far out in front of his much too-short jeans. He clutched several crumpled dollar bills in his grimy hands. The girl's clothing resembled her brother's. Her head was a matted mass of curly hair. Reminders of an evening meal showed on her small face. She carried a beautiful pair of shiny, gold house slippers. As the Christmas music sounded in the store's stereo system, the girl hummed along, off-key but happily.

When we finally approached the checkout register, the girl carefully placed the shoes on the counter as though they were a treasure. The clerk rang up the bill. "That will be $6.09," she said. The boy laid his crumpled dollars atop the stand while he searched his pockets. He finally came up with $3.12. "I guess we will have to put them back," he bravely said. "We will come back some other time, maybe tomorrow."

With that statement, a soft sob came from the little girl. "But Jesus would have loved these shoes," she cried. "Well, we'll go home and work some more," said the boy. "Don't cry. We'll come back." Quickly I handed $3 to the cashier; after all, it was Christmas. Suddenly a pair of arms came around me and a small voice said, "Thank you, lady."

"What did you mean when you said Jesus would like the shoes?" I asked. The boy answered, "Our mommy is sick and going to heaven. Daddy said she might go before Christmas to be with Jesus." The girl spoke, "My Sunday School teacher said the streets in heaven are shiny gold, just like these shoes. Won't Mommy be beautiful walking on those streets to match these shoes?" My eyes flooded as I looked into her tear-streaked face. "Yes," I answered, "I am sure she will." Silently I thanked God for sending these children to remind me of the true spirit of giving.

Jesus did about everything for us. Yes, it's true. He even died for us. Jesus did all His kind deeds and miracles for us. Remember when you do a kind act, you're doing something for Jesus.

—Jeffery Wood, age nine

One recess when I was eight, I was playing soccer and was having a wonderful time until someone kicked a ball in my face. Coming out of nowhere, my best friend came running to me like a speeding bullet. He got me an icepack and I happily returned to the field.

We are not placed on this earth to see through each other, but to see each other through.

—*William M. Kinnaird*

For thirty years I ran a high-powered public relations firm in the state capital. Our clients were politicians and well-heeled interest groups who hired us to get them good press and, more important, to build a political base for their actions. I was always proud of my reputation as a relentless and sometimes ruthless operator who could get the job done.

In practice that meant stepping on a lot of toes, and I have to admit it never really bothered me. It just seemed like the way you had to be in my line of work. About ten years ago, I hired a woman named Mary for mostly secretarial duties. Seven years ago I fired her after she caused a minor office blowup by confronting one of my account managers about his continued use of profanity. In fact, I hardly remembered her other than that she was a very religious person who objected to the foul language being used in the office.

Last year I was diagnosed with a particularly painful and insidious form of cancer. At first I received a lot of cards, calls, and flowers, but as time wore on it slowed to a trickle and then stopped altogether. After a number of unsuccessful operations and chemotherapy, it became clear to me that I was not going to live a whole lot longer. I realized that I wasn't afraid of death, but the thought of how much I had wasted my life was so debilitating I could hardly breathe.

That's when I got a call from Mary. Her father had died of the same kind of cancer, and she wanted to know if there was anything she could do to help. I was so lonely and desperate I asked her if she would visit me and she agreed immediately; she has been coming by once a week ever since. I once asked her how she could be so kind to me after I had treated her so callously, and she just dismissed it by saying, "If Jesus could forgive all our sins, I could certainly forgive you."

Life's most persistent and urgent question is, What are you doing for others?

—*Dr. Martin Luther King, Jr.*

It was snowing hard, the streets were deserted, and I was hurrying to get home in time to meet my daughter's school bus. Suddenly I skidded and got stuck in a snow bank. My wheels turning uselessly (I had no chains, of course), I sent up a silent prayer—"Lord, I need help!" I no sooner finished the thought when there was a rapping at my window. There stood a young man, with long hair and a beard, who quickly put a piece of cardboard under my back wheels to give me traction, and I was able to maneuver my way out. Before I took off, I offered him what was in my wallet—a $10 bill. "No," he said with a smile. "I don't need money. All I ask in return is that you help somebody in need." And since that day, I have.

You should be kind to the world as God has been kind to you. God created the world. There are different ways to be kind to the world, like picking up garbage. I won't tell you any more now. You think of some yourself.

—*Kara-Lynn Murphy, age seven*

Recently I realized that acts of kindness come not only from people, but from the beautiful world that God has created. It was one of those days when everything goes wrong. It started with my being late for work, on to having to face a mountain of irritated customers, computer breakdowns, short-tempered colleagues, car trouble on the interstate that found me walking to a telephone in a drenching thunderstorm without my umbrella, and ending with in a totally irrational and emotionally bruising fight with my husband.

I ran out of the house trying somehow to escape my problems, but the dark cloud just hung over me. As I walked through our neighborhood remembering all the bad things that had happened that day, the storm that had so rudely soaked me earlier began to clear. I came around a corner that overlooked a valley and was treated to one of the most beautiful sights I have ever seen. The clouds had thinned to long trailing wisps and were floating gracefully apart like some kind of celestial doorway, and the biggest full moon I had ever seen was slowly moving into view. I watched as the light from the moon passed like a hand over the valley, turning the entire rain-soaked valley into a kaleidoscope of reflected light. I started laughing and crying at the same time. Here I was mired in my own little dirt clod, yet I was so magnificently reminded by the grandeur of God's night sky that there was much more to life than what I was feeling in the moment.

You don't have to go overseas to be a missionary. You just go into your world and do your best to make a difference. Do what you can one life at a time, right here at home.

—*Bobbie Mason*

Late in the Christmas season I stopped to look at the notes still remaining on the Christmas Giving Tree standing in the center of the mall. All but one of the remaining notes listed a bicycle as the requested gift. Unfortunately, I couldn't afford a bike, so I took the remaining tag. It was for a twelve-year-old girl who NEEDED a jacket, but WANTED a cassette tape player. I decided to buy the jacket and found a bright red one for about half of my budget. As I started to turn away I noticed a big 30 percent off sign for a jogging suit and decided to add it to the jacket.

At the register, the clerk asked me if I was a member of their frequent buyers discount club; I wasn't, but when I explained what I was doing, she gave me the discount anyway.

That got me the jacket and jogging suit for less than half my budget, so I was able to buy the cassette player and a tape and still had $30 left. The Giving Tree tag had listed the girl's shoe size, and I decided to check out the sales at an athletic shoe store right across the street. I found a pair on sale for $29, but since I wasn't sure of the taste of a twelve-year-old girl I asked for help from a nearby couple on which color to get; they just happened to have a twelve-year-old daughter and told me, "Definitely white." When I took the shoes to the register I was disappointed to learn the white ones weren't on sale; however, after hearing my story the clerk decided that today, they were on sale.

In my own attempt to perform an act of kindness, I received two random acts of kindness from two different sales clerks that made it possible to give some little girl what she wanted, what she needed, and a pair of sneakers to boot. I live alone and have quiet holidays, but this Christmas morning I was filled with happiness imagining that little girl opening her presents, and I hope that the two sales clerks were thinking of the part they played in this girl's Christmas as well.

Kind words can be short and easy to speak, but their echoes are endless.

—*Mother Teresa*

I went back to Vietnam last year. I'm not really sure why I went; it just seemed terribly important that I go. When I think about it now, I think I went back to try to find some part of myself that I had lost there twenty-three years ago. I have really struggled to find a place in the world since I returned from Vietnam. I was hooked on drugs (I'm now clean and sober!), my marriage failed, my kids weren't speaking to me, I couldn't feel God in my life. So I decided to go back and see if I could get some kind of sign from God that I was still a good person.

It was a very strange trip, very disorienting. So much had changed and so much was exactly as it had been. I was there for five days, and most of the time I just wandered around in a fog to places I had spent time in, places I had fought in. On the last day I was taking a cab to the airport and the taxi driver started talking to me. He asked me if I had fought in Vietnam. When I said, "Yes," I was almost overcome with grief and shame. As I handed him the fare at the airport, he held onto my hand for a moment and said, "I was your enemy but now I am your friend."

On the flight back I felt more alive than I had in years. If that cab driver in Ho Chi Min City could hold my hand as a friend, then maybe I could be my own friend too. And if God could send me a sign that He loved me, maybe I could love myself as well. That was the turning point in my recovery.

While great brilliance and intellect are to be admired, they cannot dry one tear or mend a broken spirit. Only kindness can do this.

—John M. Drescher

My life truly has been blessed by the kindness of strangers. The other day while I was walking back to work from lunch with my head down, brooding over my own misery, I ran smack into a tiny old man coming out of a store and knocked him down. I was so embarrassed I could hardly speak. He picked himself up, smiled at me, and said, "Thank you, young lady. That's more excitement than I've had in months." This was so unexpected I burst out laughing, and he smiled again. As he was walking away he turned back to me and said, "You have a very beautiful laugh; use it often." That was the most wonderful thing anyone has ever said to me.

God gives us strength enough, and sense enough,
for every thing he wants us to do.

—*John Ruskin*

As long as I can remember I always wanted to be a physicist at a big university. I used to dream of walking across some ivy-covered campus with my books in hand, getting paid to stay on top of all the latest developments in my field, having lively interactions with the bright young students under my care, and maybe even adding my own contribution to our growing understanding of our world.

Throughout college I sacrificed my social life to study, and I did well enough to get accepted into a doctorate program, although not the one of my choosing. My graduate years were a lot harder, but still I did well, getting my doctorate in four years. Then the roof collapsed on me. I searched for a year and a half for a university position, coming close a couple of times, but nothing turned up, and I finally took a job teaching high school physics in my hometown to make ends meet.

I saw this job as a temporary stopover. In truth, I resented it terribly, and I'm sure my attitude showed. In my second year of teaching, I had a young boy as a student who immediately caught my attention. I had been warned about him because he had already been identified as a troublemaker—more interested in disrupting the classroom than in learning. But what captivated me was the quickness with which he could grasp ideas.

I kind of adopted him, forcing him to pay attention by putting him on the spot but also readily complimenting him when he put his mind into it. He ended up being my star student. At the end of the school year, I got a visit from the boy's father, who said, "I just wanted to thank you for caring enough to help my son see his potential. I don't know how you did it, but last night he told me he was going to get straight A's next year because he wanted to go to the university to study physics."

That night when I got home, I had this incredibly full and beautiful feeling in my body, and I realized that my dream of university teaching was not the work I was supposed to be doing. My work was here, in the hormone-crazed, confused world of young people; I had just been too blind to realize it.

Let us not grow weary while doing good, for in due season we shall reap if we do not lose heart.

—*Galatians 6:9*

I am a disabled, forty-six-year-old divorcée with two teenagers. We've been having a hard time making ends meet. My daughter, a sweet, timid seventeen-year-old, even quit school to work as a waitress to help out the family. I didn't want this, but teenagers can be awfully hard-headed.

This morning my daughter came in from work (she had to work the 9 P.M. to 6 A.M. shift) and told my son and me about a scruffy young couple who had come into the truck stop with a little girl of about three. Their car had broken down, and they wondered if they could stay in the diner and drink coffee till morning. My daughter said, "Yes" and, putting two and two together, figured out they were broke and hungry to boot. So she took her tips (about $13) and bought them all pancakes and eggs—with a big glass of milk for the little girl.

I thought she did a wonderful thing.
Please keep us in your prayers.

One can never pay in gratitude; one can only pay "in kind" somewhere else in life.

—*Anne Morrow Lindbergh*

I work in a grocery store that has a food court in it. A lot of homeless people who live in the area come in for drinks and food—not handouts, they pay for everything they get. One man practically lives in our store. He is always helping us out. He is a very kind and generous man who really doesn't have anyone but us to talk to and be with. In a funny kind of way we are his extended family. I don't make a lot of money, and for Christmas I was just giving homemade candy to family and friends. But one day I decided that while this man would undoubtedly like the candy, he would probably prefer cash, so I gave him a Christmas card with $5 in it.

Walking home that day I found $5 on the sidewalk. To me, that was really great. It was just a little reminder of when Jesus said: What you gave He would give back to you tenfold. I may have only found $5 that day, but the joy I received at knowing how I had made this man feel, combined with that beautiful moment reminding me of Christ's love, was well over tenfold in my book.

God gives us two hands—one to receive with and one to give with. We are not cisterns made for hoarding; we are channels made for sharing.

—*Billy Graham*

Thanks to a small miracle, my daughter's best friend is going to college. She graduated third in her class and was immediately accepted by the state university, but even living at home with her single mother and figuring in student loans, there was no way she could afford the cost of tuition and books. She was resigned to getting a job and going to night school, but someone at church heard about her plight and decided to help. After a very discreet flurry of phone calls, a small trust fund was collected through hundreds of small donations. The package containing the trust fund papers, all made out in the young woman's name and to be paid out over four years, arrived yesterday. She came by to show us and couldn't stop crying and laughing.

If you want a picture of success as heaven measures it, of greatness as God views it, don't look for the blaring bands of Broadway; listen, rather, for the tinkle of water splashing into a basin, while Christ, in humility that makes angels hold their breath, sponges the grime from the feet of his undeserving disciples.

—*Paul Rees*

Every once in a while we come across someone who seems to rest very naturally and comfortably in God's scheme of things. While it's tempting to think of such people as angels, as angelic as they appear they are actually something better: An ordinary person who has found their way and who steadfastly insists that for all they do for others, it is they who benefit most from it. Anna is one of those people.

Anna is a coal miner's daughter who grew up in rural Pennsylvania in the early part of the century. She was taught to crochet at age six. Her mother couldn't afford to buy yarn, so she saved the string that was used to wrap packages in the days before paper and plastic bags took over. From the time she can remember Anna worked. Now, at 93 years old, she is still working, crocheting afghans and wheelchair lap blankets that she gives to the patients in the local Christian Hospice Program.

"When you're in those wheelchairs," Anna said, "your legs can get really cold. I know, I've been in the hospital myself a few times, so this is something I can do to help. Besides, it keeps me busy. I need to be doing something with my hands, so I crochet."

When asked how she keeps working at her age, Anna just laughs. "People ask me that all the time and they want to know why I look so much younger than I am. I tell them it's because I eat a bag full of apples every week—maybe I should be doing ads for apple growers. Really, I think God just looks down on me and figures what I'm doing is worth doing."

Blessed is the influence of one true, loving, human soul on another.

—*George Eliot*

The first time I saw him was by accident. There was a fender-bender on the freeway, so I detoured through the city and as I drove down a side road, I saw an old man standing on the sidewalk, waving. At first I couldn't tell whom he was waving at, but as I drove by I realized he was making eye contact with the driver of each passing car and waving to all of us. It was so unusual it made me laugh. The next morning, I found myself changing my route to work so I could go by the waving man. Pretty soon it was something I really looked forward to. He'd always be there, waving, and more and more people—including myself—were waving back to him as we went by.

This went on for years. Then, on a few occasions, he wouldn't be there and I found myself worrying about him—

was he sick, had something happened? Finally, after an unusually long absence, I read a story in the local paper that the waving man had grown too old and frail to weather his early morning routine. It was like losing an old friend. I still drive by his spot and sometimes I wave at his house. I hope he knows how many morning smiles he was responsible for.

Serve wholeheartedly, as if you were serving the Lord, not men.

—*Ephesians 6:7*

Last year, when I was in seventh grade, I was involved in a toy drive for children. My mom got me to do it and I wasn't very excited about it. The only reason I was doing it was for extra credit in school. I spent day after day sorting toys and waiting for the clock to say it was time to go home. I had basketball practice the night of the wrapping, so I got to the school just a little bit late. I was stunned to find over 150 people there wrapping gifts. I started to feel good about what I had done.

All the help and goodwill that was shown that night really touched my heart. I hope that I will have the chance to do it again. The biggest surprise is that I didn't care about the extra credit anymore. To this day, I haven't turned in the sheet.

Whatever you did for one of the least of these brothers of mine, you did for me.

—*Matthew 25:40*

When you get as desperate as I was, all you can hope for is miracles. I had just lost my job due to "downsizing," got evicted because I couldn't pay the rent, and as quick as that my two children and I were on the street with nothing. I was scared; my heart was constantly beating so fast I couldn't even think straight. After a few weeks of sleeping in friends' living rooms and trying unsuccessfully to find a job, I made a sign—"Lost my job, evicted, and scared"—and parked myself at the busiest intersection I could find, just praying for a miracle.

Within minutes an old beat-up station wagon pulled over and an elderly couple asked me if I would come to dinner with them. At the restaurant we shared our life stories, and after we finished, I thanked them not only for the food but for being kind enough to listen to me. They asked how they could reach me and said they'd like to try to help me if they could.

Two days later I got a message from them telling me to come to a certain address at four o'clock. They were waiting for me when I arrived to give me the keys to a small apartment that they owned. They told me I could stay there rent-free until I found a job; to help me in my job search, they'd even arranged to have a phone hooked up that they would pay for until I was back on my feet. I think I must have been in shock, because I just stood there staring at them, when the woman turned to me and said, "Thank you, dear, for giving us this opportunity." That was it; I burst out in tears hugging them and thanking them, but I could barely get the words out, I was crying so hard.

I had grown up hearing it is better to give than to receive, but this was the first time I really understood what that meant.

You can judge how far you have risen in the scale of life by asking one question: How wisely and how deeply do I care? . . . To be Christianized is to be sensitized: Christians are people who care.

—*E. Stanley Jones*

I had an experience a few years ago that had the blessed effect of jolting me out of a twenty-year fog. I was raised a good Christian and I always attended church regularly and gave generously when asked, but the truth is I was only going through the motions. I had thrown myself into my work, and most of my thoughts and energy were focused on that.

One day I was coming out of a luncheon appointment with an out-of-town business associate, and on the sidewalk was a man who had passed out (I of course assumed he was drunk) with his head hanging over the gutter. I was about to hurry by, when my associate stopped, bent over, and moved the man back onto the sidewalk. Then he pulled out his cellular phone and called the police, telling them that this man was burning up with fever and needed to get to the hospital immediately. While we waited for the ambulance to arrive it felt like a heavy curtain had fallen away, and I felt so ashamed of myself. I resolved right there never to close my eyes and heart again.

It's no use trying to be clever—we are all clever here; just try to be kind—a little kind.

—*Dr. F. J. Foakes Jackson*

I have a kindness angel. Whenever I am out of sorts, scared, anxious, or angry, I always find myself calling this one particular friend who is a beacon of God's love. She listens so deeply and empathizes so completely that it never fails to soothe me. And her openhearted position is not just reserved for close friends. Countless times I have been with her in stores and taxicabs, in small groups and large gatherings, and watched with amazement as she extends her understanding and compassion to everyone around her. Lately, I've begun to notice that just being around her has had a dramatic impact on my own behavior. Where once I might have rushed to make a judgment, I find myself listening more intently. Where once I might have just said some superficial social thing, I find myself imagining what this person's circumstances must feel like and saying something from the heart. Suddenly people are gathering around me, too.

A gift is a precious gem in the eyes of him that hath it; wherever it turns, it prospers.

—*Proverbs 17:8*

I'm a registered nurse at a small hospital in northern New Hampshire. I recently relocated here and the adjustment has been tough.

We've had a lot of snow this winter, and when I am the first one off my shift in the morning, I go to the parking lot, scrape off my car, and then start on my coworkers' cars. My goal is to be done and gone by the time they get to their cars. The few times I haven't finished soon enough, it has prompted everyone to help everyone else. To see my coworkers all smiling and helping each other in the early morning, after a long night shift, reminds me of the reasons we are all doing what we do.

Recently, I had just finished a really stressful night and was the last one of the night shift to leave. I was thinking about having to clean my car and how tired I was when, to my surprise, I found my car all cleaned off with no one around to be thanked. I got in with a smile on my face, knowing that kindness really does breed kindness.

To give without any reward, or any notice, has a special quality of its own.

—*Anne Morrow Lindbergh*

I'm an accountant by trade, and a few years ago I offered my services to my church to help keep the books straight. One Saturday morning, while I was going over some paperwork for the church, my pastor stopped by to ask if I would do him a big favor and help out an elderly woman in the congregation whose husband had just passed away. The man had owned a small independent grocery store in town and apparently left an array of confusing accounts that had this poor woman in near panic.

I agreed and a few days later was elbow-deep in forty years of some of the most amazing account histories I will probably ever see. It seems this man had extended credit—sometimes years of credit—to just about every person in the town who was down on their luck. At first, my accountant nature made me feel appalled, then I got angry at the thought that this generous man could be so taken advantage of, but the more I sorted through his records the more interesting it became.

Some accounts would suddenly get paid off years later. Some, entered with a notation "kindness premium," would be paid off with sums far exceeding the original debt. I saw accounts written off with notes like "Mr. Henderson died last night, God rest his soul," and every December there would be a number of notations writing off debt that just said, "Merry Christmas."

When I had finally finished what seems now like a privileged journey through the heart of a true Christian, I presented my findings to his wife—there was still some $15,000 worth of uncollected debt on the books. She just smiled and said, "Let's just let that be Harold's final bequeath; he was always such a generous man, it is only fitting he be generous in death as well."

I shall pass through this world but once. If, therefore, there be any kindness I can show, or any good thing I can do, let me do it now, for I may never pass this way again.

—*from* The Magnificent Obsession

When I was working in Washington, D.C., in the '80s, I took the Metro daily and got off at the Farragut West Station. Many mornings, as I stepped onto the escalator, I could hear above me the voice of a man who stood at the top, nearly blocking the passage. He would call out, "Good Morning America," in the manner of Robin Williams in *Good Morning Vietnam.* People found it annoying—it was hard to get off in a hurry—and I, for one, wished he would just go away.

One morning during the Christmas season, I stepped onto the escalator and a beautifully lyrical a cappella version of "Joy to the World" greeted me. The familiar song was being sung in a clear tenor, and the words and music were so bright and beautiful that I felt I was hearing the carol for the first time. My heart skipped a beat and tears came to my eyes as I rode to the top, bathed in the blessing of this perfect song.

Sure enough it was the same man, standing off to the side today with his eyes closed, giving all of us a wonderful Christmas present as we stepped onto the pavement to face the workaday world. I have carried this stranger's precious gift with me since that day. I silently thank him for his kindness in giving me a memory I will always cherish—there is, indeed "Joy to the World, the Lord Has Come."

Human beings are created for the transcendent, for the sublime, for the beautiful, for the truthful . . . and all of us are given the task of trying to make this world a little more hospitable to these beautiful things.

—*Archbishop Desmond Tutu*

A few years ago when a rash of church burnings swept across the south, I was heartened to find out that local congregations, black and white, banded together to help each other. It reminded me of something that happened many years ago that made me truly understand what being a Christian meant.

I grew up in South Africa, the old South Africa, where apartheid was a way of life and racial segregation was taken for granted. I lived in a rather small community about fifty miles outside of Cape Town. One summer when racial tension was rising and people's fears and anxieties were at a peak, a local

African church was burned to the ground. That Sunday, sitting in our all-white church, I listened as our minister started to talk about what had happened. At first it seemed that his sermon was going to be a simple one about the evils of prejudice and violence, but then suddenly he looked up at the congregation and asked us if we had thought about what we, as good Christians, should do? No one spoke or moved a muscle. Then he told us that he would be at the site of the burned church the next morning to help in the rebuilding, and that anyone who wanted to join him was welcome.

The next day his was the only white face among the scores of people clearing away burned timbers. By the end of the day he was covered with ash and soot from the charred lumber, and the joke was going around that he had become African from one day of labor. The following week a few men from our church went out to join him, and each week thereafter more and more people from the congregation showed up, to help, serve cool drinks, and to pray. When the church was complete and ready to begin services, our two congregations held a joint prayer service to thank God for the gift He had delivered us in this unusual manner.

Find a need and fill it.

—*Ruth Stafford Peale*

One summer, when my brother and I were still in high school, we were lying on the front lawn bored silly. He said, "You know, old lady Henderson sure has let her yard go." Right there we hatched a plan to make a midnight gardening raid. The next day, Mrs. Henderson was standing out in her yard talking to every neighbor she saw about how some elves had transformed her overgrown garden into neatly trimmed bushes.

It was so much fun we planned a raid on another neighbor's yard a few days later. When the sun rose the day after, the hedge around the yard across the street was all trimmed and shaped. My mother must have figured out it was us, because later that day she made some comment about how the corner lot sure would look better with some flowers along the sidewalk instead of that bare patch of dirt, and later that afternoon we discovered four flats of flowers sitting in our garage just waiting for the midnight raiders.

It was great fun, and we continued for almost a month before we finally got caught—there is just no way to mow a lawn silently. Our little adventure not only brought smiles to the entire neighborhood, but people started taking better care of their yards, and we even ended up getting some gardening jobs.

Helping people takes time, and free time is a commodity most of us have in scant supply. It is probably at least partly true, for that reason, that the time we give to others is such a treasure to God.

—*Stephen Fortosis*

I have a friend who's a youth worker and is really dedicated to his high schoolers. He goes to their games, helps with homework, and lends a compassionate ear to their problems. In short, he is really there for them. In thanks, one year a group of his kids got together and made him a plaque that read, "The World's Second-Best Servant."

Pleasant words are as a honeycomb, sweet to the soul and health to the bones.

—*Proverbs 16:24*

It's amazing what effect the simplest acts can have. I am a high school English teacher. One day a student was goofing around and I snapped at him. Immediately I felt badly: his behavior certainly didn't warrant such a strong reaction. It was neither Christian nor kind of me. So a moment later, I went and kneeled down by his desk and apologized for yelling. He said nothing; I assumed he was angry at me. Later, a friend of his came up to me and told me that the boy had been amazed that I had said I was sorry—he had never even heard of an adult apologizing to a kid. For the rest of the year, I had no problems with that boy.

You cannot do a kindness too soon, because you never know how soon it will be too late.

—*Ralph Waldo Emerson*

My son Russ was recently killed in a car accident at age fifteen. I am writing this story in remembrance of him. At age fourteen, he was visiting his grandparents, who live in a retirement community in Denver. Russ was coming out of the parking garage when he found a billfold with $300 in cash. He told his grandparents and they found the owner. The old gentleman whose wallet it was wrote Russ a thank-you note and enclosed $30, saying that he was eternally grateful because Russ' action had restored his faith in the youth of today.

Very early in the morning, while it was still dark, Jesus got up, left the house and went to a solitary place, where he prayed.

—*Mark 1:35*

I was driving home the other day, listening to the radio, and a guy was talking about kindness. He mentioned how easy it is to let it slip out of our lives, because we are all in such a hurry we rush through each day without ever really seeing other people, much less helping them. His advice was to start every day with a ritual to open ourselves up to what we will encounter during the day.

That thought really struck me, because just a week earlier the sermon at church had been about starting the day with God. I realized the man on the radio and the pastor were both talking about the same thing and resolved to begin the next morning. After getting ready for work, I sat down in a sunny alcove in my house, thanked God for all I had been given, and tried to let my heart open up. It was one of the best days I'd had in a long time. Everything and everybody just seemed so crystal clear. Though I usually eat lunch at my desk, this day I went out with one of my coworkers and had a great conversation. I even had a very brief but wonderful exchange with an elderly man while standing in line at the grocery store.

It wasn't anything dramatic, but by the time I got home I was just beaming. The whole world suddenly felt so much more wonderful.

A generous man will prosper; he who refreshes others will himself be refreshed.

—*Proverbs 11:25*

I am the activity director at a nursing home in a small town in Canada. We hold two annual bazaars, the proceeds of which fund all of the activities our residents enjoy throughout the year. Many months of preparations by residents, volunteers, and staff lead up to these events. Recently, the night of a very successful bazaar, the money that we had raised was stolen. Our dreams were shattered!

Little did we know that word of our devastation would ripple throughout the community and cause people to whip into action. Local merchants organized an auction, service groups donated money, individuals arrived at our doorstep with cash and checks. The most heartrending act was by a six-year-old girl who emptied her piggy bank and brought in the contents. We were overwhelmed by this support—all of the money that was stolen and more was replaced.

A kind deed a day, like little drops of rain, makes a mighty ocean.

—*Lim Hsiu Mei*

A fifth-grade boy writes: My act of kindness is small but pretty good. Every day, say at least one kind thing to everyone you talk to. This isn't hard to do and it makes God, you, and the people you talk to feel good.

We are not sent into the world to do anything into which we cannot put our hearts.

—*John Ruskin*

Meeting people has always been hard for me. I'm very shy, and when I meet people I get all bottled up, so my words don't come out easily. I was always the one who was standing around by herself at parties. The older I got the more I started to feel sorry for myself, like I had been thrown into the world with this huge character flaw that was going to doom me to a long lonely existence. My attitude got so bad I didn't even want to be around myself.

I desperately needed to do something, so I volunteered at an elderly care home a few blocks from where I lived. An amazing thing happened—suddenly I was surrounded by people who smiled at me, wanted to talk to me, and were excited when I showed up. I volunteered there for a year and then was hired on staff and have been there ever since. Now

I'm surrounded by warm wonderful friends and feel like the luckiest person in the world. When I think back to how I got here, it seems like my loneliness was really just the vehicle God gave me to get me where I needed to be.

The greatest sermons I have ever heard were not preached from pulpits, but from sickbeds.

—*M. R. DeHaan*

I was in my mid-twenties, returning home on a flight from the East Coast after burying my father, who had died at the age of forty-nine from lung cancer. It had been a very difficult time. I had known Dad was sick for some time, but my own anxiety about illness and death had me twisted in knots—I kept putting off visiting him until it was too late. He was gone before I got there. I was doubting the existence of God—how could He have let this happen? My father was too young to die! Now, all I wanted was to be left alone to my thoughts. So of course I ended up on a full flight sitting next to a man about my age who obviously wanted to talk.

At first I resisted his attempts to get a conversation going, giving one-word answers, avoiding eye contact, looking like I was really interested in my in-flight magazine. But it was useless. Then he told me very matter-of-factly that he was on his way home to die. I guess I kind of recoiled at that so he said, "Don't worry, it isn't contagious." Somewhat to my own amazement I heard the words "Are you scared?" come out of my mouth. Normally I would never have been so direct, but my own experience had really affected me. Anyway, that certainly broke the ice and we ended up deep in conversation throughout the remainder of the flight.

I don't know how to describe it, but it was such a liberating experience for me. This guy was no hero and no saint. He was scared, he was confused, he was worried about how he would handle dying, but through it all he was determined to at least face what was happening to him as honestly and courageously as possible. At one point, I got up the nerve to ask, "Aren't you mad at God for letting you die so young?" He looked me straight in the eye and in the most tender voice said, "I can feel God's love around me all the time now. I have no room for anger. Only love." As he spoke those words, a wave of love and peace washed over me. I knew now my father was at peace, surrounded by God's loving presence.

My children, love must not be a matter of words or talk; it must be genuine, and show itself in action. This is how we may know that we belong to the realm of truth.

—1 John 3:18–19

One of my heroes was Mother Teresa. Just the idea that someone could give up so much for a lifetime of service in the slums of Calcutta seems so much bigger than I can ever be. I read an interview once during which she was asked this same question: How could she sacrifice so much? Her answer surprised me. She said it was a very silly question; her work was not about sacrifice at all, it was a sacred privilege that she had been given.

At the time I was barely squeaking by, a single mother with two small boys and a job that wasn't paid terribly well, but I wanted in my own small way to try this thing Mother Teresa was talking about. So I sat my boys down, and we decided to try to save $150 over the next four weeks by cutting out trips to McDonald's, eating more frugally, and just not buying anything we didn't absolutely need. We even did some investigation and found out about a family in our church that was going through very hard times, and we decided to give the money to them anonymously when we reached our goal.

It ended up taking almost six weeks but we made it, and, more important, it was a privilege. Just the experience of planning meals that were inexpensive, getting gleeful assistance from two boys who usually flee at the mention of chores, trying to duplicate the taste of a Big Mac at home, and the weekly ritual of deciding how much we could put aside from that week was enough to convince me.

God does not comfort us to make us comfortable,
but to make us comfort others.

—Dr. Jowett

I worked for three years on a hospital ward for cancer and terminally ill patients on Long Island. We had admitted a young homeless woman who was in the final stages of AIDS. She was obstinate, noncompliant, demanding, and obnoxious. All of us went out of our way to avoid her, during visiting hours she received no one, and no next of kin was listed on her chart.

One Sunday morning during the change of shift, I was watching as the incoming nurse was going through her charts and making notes. She stopped, read a chart, smiled, got up, and walked to the back room where other staff was on break. I watched as she pointed to something on a chart. Then she closed the chart and rushed downstairs.

A few minutes later, she returned, carrying a big cardboard cake box containing a beautifully decorated ice cream cake with pink writing on it. She gathered up every nurse, secretary, supervisor, and aide and announced it was our least favored patient's birthday. She wanted us to all go in, sing "Happy Birthday," and present the cake.

We entered the patient's dimly lit room. She sat in bed thin, fragile, and slightly contorted to one side with the blankets pulled almost up to her eyes. As we began to sing, she slowly dropped the blanket. She sat straight, smiled, and then began to sob. I realized that this would probably be her last birthday, and this act of kindness might well be the greatest gift she'd ever received.

Small service is true service. . . . The daisy, by the shadow that it casts, protects the lingering dewdrop from the sun.

—*William Wordsworth*

It is written in Isaiah that "a little child shall lead them." Boy, is that ever true when it comes to my own kids. Last Saturday, I was working in the kitchen when my two youngsters came running in, absolutely glowing with happiness. My daughter, the youngest at four years old, blurted out, "Mommy, Mommy, we carried Mrs. Gertz' groceries in for her; she asked us and we did it!" They were so happy about having helped my elderly neighbor with her groceries, you would have thought someone had just promised them a trip to Disneyland.

I know that helping others is always rewarding to me, but sometimes I just know it in my head; somehow that wonderful feeling of being your best self gets lost in the daily routine. Standing there looking at their happy faces brought it all back so strongly.

Few of the valuable things in life "just happen." When they happen it is because we recognize their importance and devote ourselves to them.

—*Alan Loy McGinnis*

I heard a preacher on the radio once say that the original word for *sinning* was literally translated as "missing the mark." I'm a dancer; in dance, your "mark" is the place on the dance floor you are supposed to be at any given moment in the dance. That idea of sin really struck me. It started me thinking about my own life in a different way, and I realized that for me life really is like an incredibly complicated dance. The idea that sin isn't just a litany of bad things you can do, but the failure to do what you should be doing at that moment really fascinated me.

I started to change the way I acted; I suddenly began feeling myself moving through this dance, in the grocery store, at work, even when I was doing the most mundane things like driving my car. And I found myself becoming a much nicer person in many small ways, smiling more, being willing to interact more with other people, helping people out. It seems my "mark" keeps drawing me out toward other people, and I have never been this happy before.

The power of love and caring can change the world.

—*James Autry*

One day some friends had come over to share lunch,and we started talking about all the kind things that had happened to us in our lives. Story after incredible story came out, and you could feel the presence of a beautiful grace settling all around us. We were all sitting there tingling with these funny grins on our faces when one of my friends suggested that maybe we were all here for a reason.

After a little excited discussion we decided to spend the next half-hour together in silent prayer for a family that had recently been in the news because of a very traumatic tragedy. It was such a beautiful experience that we decided to get together regularly for long-distance anonymous prayer sessions.

The nicest thing we can do for our heavenly Father is to be kind to one of His children.

—*Saint Teresa of Avila*

It was Mother's Day. My wonderful, lively sons, age three and five, were begging to go to the park. I was tired, lonely, and a little depressed. There was no one to make a fuss over me—my husband and I had recently separated, I was living in Australia and my family was all back in the States, and the boys were too young to understand. We had no car, little money, no luxuries.

As we headed for the park, we passed a florist shop. It was doing a brisk business. I stood still for a moment, clutching a small hand in each of mine, and looked at the lovely floral displays spilling out onto the sidewalk. Then with a shrug and fighting back a few tears, I walked on down the street.

Half a block later, I heard footsteps running up behind us. A voice said, "Excuse me, Miss." I turned around to see a young man of nineteen or twenty, out of breath, clutching a large bouquet of carnations. “Happy Mother’s Day,” he said, thrusting the bouquet into my hands, and ran back into the shop. I just stood there for several minutes, tears flowing freely now, marveling at this gift of love from a strange, young angel.

To love abundantly is to live abundantly.

—*Anonymous*

We had a big party for my grandmother's ninetieth birthday. Almost the entire extended family showed up, and one by one we all drifted over to talk to her. But by time I got my turn, I had already gotten reports from my upset relatives that all she would talk about was how tired she was and how she wanted to die. When I finally got to talk to her, she started telling me that she thought God must have gotten awfully busy and forgotten about her, because she just knew she wasn't supposed to still be alive. After all, she said, her husband was long dead, all her friends were gone, and her body was just one constant set of aches and pains.

It hurt me to hear her talking like that, because I loved her so much and didn't want her ever to die, but the more she talked the more sense she made, and I found myself understanding what I thought I would never understand. I realized that I was looking out across our yard at her six children, their spouses, eighteen grandchildren, and five great-grandchildren, all gathered to honor her. I turned to her and pointed at everyone, and said, "God didn't forget you, he just didn't want you to leave without saying goodbye to all those people who will still be here and will always love you."

At that she smiled, pulled herself to her feet, and said, "You're such a smart girl; let's make it a great party."

A friend always loves, and a brother is born to share trouble.

—*Proverbs 17:17*

Recently something happened that taught me that listening well is an act of kindness—to myself as well as to the person I'm listening to. I was having coffee with a friend one day, and sat there hunched over my cup, preoccupied with a long list of problems that seemed unsolvable. Suddenly my friend said, "You haven't heard a thing I've said." To my complete embarrassment, I realized it was true. I stood up, shook my whole body, sat down, took a few deep breaths and said, "OK, I'm really sorry; I'm listening now." It was kind of a joke, but it worked. I suddenly found it very easy to be really focused on what she was saying.

We talked for a while longer, and when I left I realized that just listening, really listening and responding to her tale of woe, had made *me* feel so much better. My problems were still there, but they didn't seem so urgent anymore. I knew that for her, being able to share what was going on in her life had helped her as well. Nothing really had changed, but in some strange way, on some deeper level, everything had changed.

It is more blessed to give than to receive.

—*Acts of the Apostles 20:35*

Often it is those who have the least who take most to heart Jesus' words to be kind to your neighbor. The other day as I was going into a fast-food restaurant, there was a homeless man standing outside asking for money. I bought an extra hamburger and went back outside to give it to him before returning to eat my own lunch. I saw out the window that he had started to unwrap the burger and then had noticed something across the street; he stopped, rewrapped the burger, and left. Curious, I walked over to the window and watched as he crossed the street and, with a flourish and a bow, gave the hamburger to a homeless woman with a small child who was sitting on the sidewalk.

Grace gives without the receiver realizing how great the gift really is.

—*Rebecca Manley Pippert*

My family had just moved to Texas where I had gotten a job teaching. By the time we got there we were completely broke and were facing our first Christmas in Texas with a total budget of just over $4. Somehow the staff and teachers at the school figured this all out, and a few weeks before Christmas I got a message that the principal wanted to see me. My first reaction was, "Oh God, what now, I don't need any more trouble in my life."

But when I got there, he handed me an envelope with money in it and told me that everyone had wanted to help welcome me and that he hoped I would accept it for the gift of caring that it was. As if that wasn't enough, he pulled out a bag with already wrapped presents for my children. That was such a beautiful act of grace; it will stay with me forever.

If anyone says, "I love God," and hates his brother, he is a liar; for he who does not love his brother whom he has seen, cannot love God whom he has not seen.

—1 John 4:21

I was away from home and family, working on my doctorate at Duke University in the '60s. Another Christian student and I were belittled for our Christian faith. Once someone broke into my friend's room; when he returned he found beer cans stacked around the room and pornographic pictures plastered on the walls and ceiling.

On my dorm floor, a group of medical students would regularly go out drinking late at night. After midnight they'd pound loudly on my door and shout obscenities. I'd lie in the dark praying, but with growing resentment in my heart.

I was home one weekend wondering what to do. During my quiet time, I read Luke 6:27: "Love your enemies. Be kind to those who hate you." Love those jerks? I couldn't stand them, but I prayed God would not only change my attitude but maybe even the attitude of my dormmates.

I brought back from home a box of my wife's chocolate chip cookies and took them across the hall to the ringleader. He looked shocked to see me at his door. "My wife baked a batch of cookies and I thought you'd like some." Struck speechless, he took the box, mumbling something I assumed was a "Thank you." The bashing on my door and the obscenities stopped from that day on.

Beloved, let us love one another: for love is of God; and every one that loveth is born of God.

—*1 John 4:7*

I was driving home from work one day and saw a small truck about half a mile ahead swerve and then suddenly flip over onto the side of the road. My stomach instantly knotted up and, as I approached, I saw with growing disbelief at least forty cars speed past without stopping. I too found myself wanting desperately to keep going to put distance between myself and that smashed truck. But something would not allow me to flee. I knew that I would not be able to live with myself if I passed by.

Nervous and scared at what I might find, I pulled over and ran to the partially opened door. Inside, a young man, bleeding from his head, was trying to climb out. As I reached in to help him, I saw a woman's arm coming in from behind me to turn off the engine. Across the cabin, another man was leaning in to help undo the driver's safety belt. Together we eased the young man out of the car while another woman called an ambulance on her car phone. The four of us stayed and did what we could for the injured man until the ambulance arrived. As it was driving away, I looked around me and there were almost a dozen anxious faces staring back at me.

It was then I realized that we who are trying to live as God wants us to are not alone; that, contrary to what it looks like on television and in the newspaper, we are a part of a vast network of well-intentioned people seeking the good and loving well.

If we do not radiate the light of Christ around us, the sense of the darkness that prevails in the world will increase.

—*Mother Teresa*

I worked for an insurance company for five years while I was going to school at night. It was a very difficult and stressful time of my life, made infinitely worse by the committed pettiness of the company. We lived by production quotas and the time clock; we even had to clock out and in for our breaks. The whole office of about forty people was just beaten down by the cruel regimen, except for one woman who I swear brought us all through each day.

She was the most cheerful person I've ever met. Fortunately for us, her job was to drop off and pick up the files we were supposed to be churning out, so she passed by all of our desks several times a day. No matter what, she walked through that office like a radiant beam of sunshine on a heavily overcast day. I don't know how she came by such a joyful disposition, but I for one never would have made it through those days without her.

The great thing in this world is not so much where we are, but in what direction we are moving.

—Oliver Wendell Holmes

My senior year in high school was a very tough time for me. I was messing up my life right and left, getting into fights with my parents almost every day, barely passing classes, staying out late drinking, and hanging around with a bunch of troublemakers. The strange thing was, I knew I was screwing up and I wanted to stop, but it was almost as if I didn't care enough about my own life, or maybe I just thought it was already too late.

The one really good thing in my life at that time was cross-country running. When I could just take off and run and run, it made me feel so free, like I was leaving everything behind. At the biggest meet of the year, I ended up in a two-man battle with a guy named Jason from our rival high school. Toward the end of the race I put on a burst and got out in front of him by about ten yards, and then my foot caught on something and I went slamming to the ground.

While I was lying there trying to catch my breath, I realized that Jason had stopped and was trying to help me back onto my feet. Without saying a word, we started off again. I was still trying to get my breathing under control and running pretty slow, but Jason just ran beside me. We finished the race side by side.

That dramatic stumble and the kindness Jason showed me put things into perspective for me. It was just what I had needed. After that, getting my life back on track didn't seem all that hard.

God, help us to enter into the troubles of others, know them as if they were our own, and act accordingly.

—*Avery Brooke*

I was visiting the Vietnam Veterans' Memorial during my sophomore year in college. I spent a few hours talking to volunteers and people passing by. It wasn't until late afternoon that I noticed a man who was sitting on a bench facing the Memorial, calmly observing people as they walked from the wall. His canes were lying on the bench beneath him and his jacket rested across his knees. He had only one leg. His calm stare seemed to reach out to a memory, some distant anger he was struggling to hide. I was about to pass him by when I caught him glancing at me. Even though I was intimidated, I walked up and introduced myself.

My fears were eased by his warm welcome. We talked for some time about our families, friends, and favorite pastimes.

As the early signs of dusk reflected in deep reds and golden hues from the wall, I sensed he wanted to speak about the war and the loss of his leg. Finally, he looked at me with hesitation and said in a troubled voice, "I know where his name is, I know which panel, the line and the exact location, but I can't bring myself to do it. I'm nothing compared to him. I can't face him. I can't let myself remember and I certainly can't see my pitiful reflection in that wall. He should have lived. He deserved to come home. I wish it were my name on that wall. It's my place—I inspired his eagerness to be a hero."

I took his hand in mine and held it tightly as he wept. Somehow I knew I couldn't part from this man without making sure he touched the wall. I said to him in a steady voice, "I'll go with you." I gathered up his canes and helped him get his balance. Then we slowly walked down the wall together. No words were spoken between us as we solemnly passed by the names of honored heroes. Finally he paused in front of a panel and reached out his hand. I felt this was his private moment, and I looked away. I knew he needed to see his own reflection in the wall.

As he leaned forward to rest his head on the wall, tears streamed down his face and he put his arms around me for balance. I cried with him. He saw my tears and held me close, saying, "He was my brother, you know, and in my mind he's still twenty years old."

As we parted he kissed me respectfully on each side of my face. We didn't exchange addresses or phone numbers, but before he left, he turned around and said, "If you need to remember me, my name is Sean and you can find me forever in the reflection of that wall."

Let us not be justices of the peace, but angels of peace.

—*Saint Therese of Lisieux*

My father was a police detective. After he retired, he agreed to help out with security for a large grocery store that was having trouble with shoplifters. One day he caught a young boy of about ten. He asked the youngster to empty his pockets. Along with the shoplifted items out came the boy's pet hamster. My dad asked why he had the pet in his pocket. The child explained that he didn't have a cage for it.

After giving the boy a lecture on shoplifting, my dad had the boy promise to return the next day to do some chores at the store for punishment. When the boy returned, Dad gave him an old birdcage from our attic for his hamster. I'm sure my father's act of understanding and generosity did more than the punishment to deter future petty crime.

Make yourself necessary to someone.

—*Ralph Waldo Emerson*

I've always been a classic "type A" personality, moving at light speed and cramming as much as possible into each day. A few years ago I was brought to a screeching halt when my back went out on me. One minute I was standing in the kitchen throwing a quick meal together before heading back to work, and the next minute I was lying on the linoleum unable to move. The worst part was that even after I did all the things I was supposed to do—muscle relaxers, chiropractic treament, massage—I only improved to the point where I could move around. The slightest bit of stress would send my back into another spasm.

After about three weeks of moping around worrying that this was never going to change, I had a visit from a woman at my church. She introduced herself, told me that she had heard about my back problems and that she had gone through a similar experience, and then offered to show me a few exercises that had worked for her. I was both grateful for the gesture and skeptical at the same time, but after a very relaxed hour on my living room floor my back definitely felt better, and just talking to this woman had raised my spirits.

For a couple of months she continued to drop by and do exercises with me and we'd talk about anything and everything. As active as I was, I had never really paid much attention to my body and my health, and I learned from her to pay more attention and give more respect to this beautiful vessel God had provided for me. Because of this one person's kindness, the "tragedy" of my back turned into a major blessing in my life.

If a person isn't loving and kind, it shows that he doesn't know God—for God is love.

—1 John 4:8

When I was younger, I dated a woman for about six months, and really acted like a jerk. I wasn't in love with her but I had nothing else going on, so I just kept seeing her. The longer it went on, the worse I acted. It was as if I didn't have the courtesy to tell her she didn't mean anything to me, but was unconsciously trying to show her by treating her like dirt.

One night, after spending only a couple of hours with her, I left and ended up running out of gas out in the middle of nowhere. As I sat there hoping someone would come by, I kept thinking that I really deserved to be stranded for acting so badly. I waited for almost half an hour and then an old Rambler went by, slowed down, and backed up. Inside was a little, gray-haired old lady. It really surprised me that she'd stopped since we were way off the main road, it was nearing midnight, and she didn't know me from Adam. She drove me fifteen miles to the all-night gas station and then back again—it was probably one in the morning by time she was back on her own way. As she drove off, she called out the window, "Remember son, God loves you!"

She'll never know it, but that old lady in the Rambler was a turning point in my life. I figured that if she could treat so kindly someone she had never met before, I could at least not mistreat someone I knew well.

We are not made for law, we are made for love.

—*George Macdonald*

Reading about the trial of the man responsible for blowing up the Oklahoma City Federal Building had a very strange effect on me. On the one hand it was such a horrible, inhuman thing for anyone to do that it was simply beyond my comprehension how so much hate could find its way into one person. But what disturbed me even more was the parade of victims' family members clambering to testify at the penalty phase of the trial to demand that this man be put to death.

I suppose I could understand the unbelievable hurt and anger, but it still disturbed me in a way I couldn't shake. A few months later I read another story about a woman in California who had made a plea with the Governor's Office to commute the death sentence on a man who had murdered her daughter fifteen years earlier. She said she had been called by God to meet this man face to face in prison, and after a series of meetings she was convinced that his execution would be a great wrong. Reading that story rekindled my hope that we can indeed overcome evil with love.

Enter through the narrow gate. For wide is the gate and broad is the road that leads to destruction, and many enter through it. But small is the gate and narrow is the road that leads to life, and only a few find it.

—*Matthew 7:13–14*

I'm an attorney in a medium-sized law firm. I've always enjoyed my work and I get along well with most of the people in the office. Jack was the one guy I couldn't quite figure out. He sort of stood outside the social circle, very reserved, didn't really participate in office gossip, and rarely showed up at our nightly watering hole. Everyone respected him for his work, but his claim to fame around the office was that he was always pushing us to do more pro bono work.

A while back I was going through a difficult spell with my thirteen-year-old daughter, and it must have spilled over into work, because one evening Jack came into my office and asked if I was all right. It caught me by surprise and I said something off-handed about trying to figure my daughter out. He smiled and said, "Now there is a challenge worth worrying about."

We ended up talking for about an hour, and his concern and wisdom really turned things around for me. I'd been trying to analyze my daughter like a good attorney, but after our talk I realized our relationship had nothing at all to do with anything rational. It was all about feelings, and in that arena I was really a rank beginner. Jack gave me a few suggestions that worked amazingly well. Driving home that evening I felt better than I had in years, and I realized that this was the first time in my life I had really had a heart-to-heart talk with another father about what was so important to me. Jack was definitely different, and I thank God that I was fortunate enough to get to know him.

For finally, we are as we love. It is love that measures our stature.

—*William Sloane Coffin*

I play the organ for my church, and last week I had the occasion to witness something that reminded me how easy it is to forget what is really important in life. I played at two funerals in one day; the one in the morning was for one of the richest and most powerful men in the county. The one in the afternoon was for a very sweet old lady who lived in one of the poorest sections of town.

The morning funeral was very sparsely attended, whereas the afternoon funeral had people spilling out all the doors. After the service people milled around in the courtyard exchanging stories about the thousands of little ways this woman had impacted their lives.

Talent develops itself in solitude; character in the stream of life.

—*Johann Wolfgang von Goethe*

Our church sponsors a scholarship that is given each year to the graduating senior with the highest grade-point average. Throughout high school, my best friend Jody and I would trade off leading our class. When the final grades were in, I had won the scholarship by a fraction of a percent. I was very happy since the scholarship meant I would be able to go to the college I really wanted to attend, but I felt badly about Jody because she needed it just as much as I did. I had been notified of the scholarship by mail, and of course I wanted to tell Jody, but I was also uncertain about how to do it.

Finally I got up my courage and drove over to her house. She responded with such unrestrained enthusiasm that I said, "But I thought you wanted to win." I'll never forget what she replied. "Of course I did, but I didn't get it and you did, and I'm so happy for you. I'll find a way to go somehow." I couldn't help it; I just started crying right there on the spot. She was so kind to put her own wants aside to rejoice with me.

Do things for others and you'll find your self-consciousness evaporating like morning dew on a Missouri cornfield in July.

—*Dale Carnegie*

I don't know about other people, but I found my high school years to be really hard. By the time I was a senior I was so wrapped up in my own problems (which of course seemed really huge) that I was a royal pain to be around. In fact that's exactly what my father said when he lowered the boom on me. He said I had lost track of what was important and that I had to spend the summer doing some kind of volunteer work, or he was not going to pay my way to college.

This came as somewhat of a shock to me since I had very different plans for the summer, but my father didn't leave me much choice about the matter. I worked as a volunteer camp counselor for a local church group that brings inner-city and disadvantaged kids up to the mountains for the summer. I had an absolute blast with the kids. They'd come off the bus so excited and bursting with energy it was contagious. That summer was one of the best in my life, and it definitely helped change my perspective.

So in everything, do unto others what you would have them do unto you.

—*Matthew 7:12*

One day at school a girl in my class tripped and spilled her backpack onto the ground. The wind started blowing papers all around, and most of the kids laughed really hard. I started to laugh too, but then I remembered that in Sunday School I learned we should treat people the way we want to be treated. So I stopped laughing and helped her pick up her papers. She smiled at me and said, "Thank you."

Our brightest blazes of gladness are kindled by unexpected sparks.

—*Samuel Johnson*

I'm an old lady. One day, I was sitting alone on a bench waiting for the bus to Monterey, where our church was having a yard sale, and enjoying the gorgeous day. I noticed a young man about a block away walking toward me. Then I remembered the bus would be there shortly and I'd better have my money ready. As I was getting out my change purse, a shadow fell over me, and I saw this man's feet in front of me. Fear jumped in—would I be mugged? Attacked? I looked up to see him slightly bent toward me saying, "And a good morning to you," as he held out an African Daisy for me. I was so shocked all I could do was say, "Thank you," as he went on his way.

The more kindness you give away, the richer your life will become.

—*Tang Tuck Wing*

When I pray, I always try to listen for what God wants me to do. One day, when I was in the process of moving to a new town, God spoke to me and told me I should give my washing machine to a large family in need. At first, I tried to ignore the request. I didn't have money for a new washer. But it really did seem the right thing to do, so I called up the family and arranged for them to pick up the washer before I moved. They were so happy it was well worth it. When I got to the new town, I searched and searched for a place to rent that I could afford. It was hard because the rental market was tight. But finally I found a little place—and guess what? It had a washer and a dryer!

A good heart is better than all the heads in the world.

—*Edward Lytton*

When I was in high school my best friend was a girl named Anna. For three years we were inseparable. At the time it was the most important relationship in my life, because we really shared our hopes and dreams and had lots of fun in the process. When we were seniors, Anna started hanging out with a crowd of kids that was very heavily into drinking, and she was getting wilder and wilder, staying out all night, even passing out from too much drinking. At first I tried to ignore it and even helped make excuses for her, but finally I realized that if I was really her friend I needed to say something to her.

Looking back, I'm pretty sure I didn't do a very good job of it, because I was scared and angry and I probably came across way too harshly. We had a big fight and that was the end of our friendship. For years I used to replay that conversation in my mind and think of all the things I could have done differently, but eventually it receded and I didn't think about her that much anymore. But occasionally a song on the radio or something someone would say would bring her back into my mind, and it always made me feel so sad.

Last year, in the middle of a very hectic schedule, I got a letter from her—fifteen years later. It was short and to the point; she said that she felt badly that she had let so much time go by without telling me that I had been a real friend. The tears just started flowing. I couldn't believe how strong an impact that letter had on me.

Sow the seeds of kindness and reap the harvest of happiness.

—*Chua Guat Mui*

I have always believed that when we are presented with an opportunity to show kindness to someone, the world is giving us a gift that is its own reward. So when I found myself on a long intercontinental flight sitting next to a young woman with two small restless children, I dove right in. We had a great time and eventually the kids fell asleep.

As the young woman and I sat talking, I suddenly began feeling lightheaded and then increasingly uncomfortable. At one point, she reached over and touched my forehead and said, "You are burning up." I had gotten the flu—and was feeling worse and worse. Through the rest of the trip she took care of me, cooling me down with a damp washcloth, helping me back and forth to the bathroom, and keeping my spirits up with her genuine concern. It was both the worst and the best flight I have ever taken.

Kindness is a language which the dumb can speak, the deaf can understand.

—*C. N. Bovee*

Recently I spent a year and a half traveling around the world on a tiny budget. When I returned, many of my friends expressed amazement that I could have done it, saying, "How could you get by in all those countries when you didn't have money and you didn't know the languages?"

Every time I was asked that question, my mind would be flooded with hundreds of memories of all the people I had met who had so enthusiastically helped me each and every time I needed assistance: The little Japanese woman who led me eight blocks out of her way to an address I never could have found by myself; the Indian family who shared their sack of fresh fruit with me on the ship from Mombassa to Bombay; the old Thai woman who brought me buckets of ice and the most delicious soups as I sweated through a three-day fever in her small hotel;

the African man who guided me up Mount Kilimanjaro and back in one day; the hundreds of people I met on trains, buses, and street corners who shared their smiles and greetings.

It is amazing how easy it was. The lack of ability to communicate verbally was no obstacle. Somehow we always made ourselves understood. Kindness, like God's love, is a universal language.

The only justification for looking down on somebody is to pick him up.

—*Reverend Jesse Jackson*

For years, every time I went to the grocery store, I passed a homeless woman who seemed to be living on a bench in front of the store. She never said anything to me, but she was dirty, and I felt threatened by her. At first I would hurry past her, but then it started to bother me. I was angry at her for being there, but I was also upset with myself for getting so flustered.

Gradually I began to give her whatever loose change I had. One day I stopped and talked to her just long enough to introduce myself and learn her name. After that we would always smile and greet each other by name. I actually began to look forward to seeing her smile and hearing her ask me how I was doing.

One day I sat with her for a while, and she told me a little about her life and how she had gotten to this place. She told me it was people like me—people who were still willing to see her as a person—who gave her the strength to keep trying. It was around Thanksgiving and she said, "Last year, I didn't have anything to be thankful for. But this year, I thank God for you."

See everything. Overlook a great deal. Improve a little.

—Pope John XXIII

I don't want to tell the story of my childhood. I've done it enough already. I know how painful it was, and now all I want to do is keep working to put the pieces of my life together.

But there is one part of the story I will always want to talk about. The day I met Claire. When I met her, I was at the very bottom and looked it—without home, without hope, and without the energy to care anymore. Her job was to scour the streets for the castoffs of society and try to help them. It was her mission as a Christian, she said. She found me and took me under her wing, getting me food and temporary shelter but, more important, treating me with respect even though I was the last person to think I deserved it.

She never lectured me and never preached to me; she was always just warm and friendly and encouraging. She treated me like I was a human being and, to my own surprise, I started to believe it was true. No one had ever been so nice to me. For me that was the real beginning of my life. This year, on the anniversary of the day she dragged me off the streets, I went back to the church shelter she works at, with balloons and a huge birthday cake, and threw myself a party.

The world cannot always understand one's profession of faith, but it can understand service.

—*Ian Maclaren*

The story I want to tell was passed down in my family from my great-grandfather. He was a young captain from Pennsylvania fighting in the Civil War. In preparation for a coming battle he had requisitioned a beautiful Georgia plantation home as a field hospital. He told the lady of the house to leave before the battle started, but she replied, "I am a Christian woman. I am staying. There will be wounded and I can be useful." For four days, her land was occupied by the enemy and turned into a bloody battlefield while she tirelessly did everything she could to ease the suffering of the wounded and dying Union soldiers. Word of her caring spread through the troops, and when they were leaving, every man turned and saluted as they passed her home.

My great-grandfather said that it was the most enduring memory he had of that horrible war, because it reminded him that even in the midst of an incredibly brutal and savage experience, one person's simple kindness could still shine through.

My little children, let us not love in word or in tongue, but in deed and in truth. And by this we know that we are of the truth, and shall assure our hearts before Him.

—*1 John 3:18*

I was raised by parents who really believed that life was about service—service to God and service to mankind. That's why, I think, that when I became an adult believing in the good and continuing on even when I was discouraged came naturally to me. But recently the constant battering of bad news and a series of personal setbacks finally pushed me into a state of despair. As much as I wanted to believe things would improve, as much as I desperately wanted to believe that in time we can turn our troubled world into a joyful paradise, I was on the verge of giving up.

Then one day, when I was getting out of my car, I saw a little boy leaning over a bird in my next-door neighbor's yard.

The bird had flown into a plate glass window and injured itself, and the boy was building a small nest in a shoe box to take the bird home and care for it. Seeing him tenderly lift that bird was like the ringing of a bell. I realized that caring is a part of all of us. Like that small boy, we all move through life with the love of God in our hearts. We may lose track, get too busy and too distracted to pay attention, get bogged down in the day-to-day troubles of life, but love is always there, ready to be awakened.

Let love be your greatest aim.

—1 Corinthians 14:1

There is a place in the heart of America that is dedicated to prayer, prayer for anyone and everyone who calls or writes in asking for help. The idea grew out of the experience of a midwestern couple, Myrtle and Charles Filmore, more than a hundred years ago. Myrtle discovered she had TB and, inspired by a single phrase from the Bible, she began to pray. Within two years she had cured herself. Intrigued by the power of prayer, the Filmores started a prayer circle that gathered regularly to pray for those in need.

By 1920 these growing bands of prayer circles had become the volunteer-staffed Silent Unity. Today it has grown into a powerful international network that operates twenty-four hours a day, taking telephone calls from people all over the world. Callers are asked their first names only. They share their grief and pain and are then joined in prayer by volunteers who ask them to turn their suffering over to God in prayer, to turn to God and know that His guidance is working through them as they seek the silent place within their souls.

Last year over a million and a half people telephoned Silent Unity for prayers. In addition, the organization received tens of thousands of letters. At the headquarters of Silent Unity just outside Kansas City, a dome sits over the prayer chapel that is illuminated day and night to remind passersby that prayer is always in session. Participants visit the chapel in regular sessions to pray for those who have written and called asking for help. Twice a day, at the morning and evening shift changes, the staff gathers in the chapel for group prayer.

In a further experiment with the awesome power of prayer, Unity began a World Day of Prayer four years ago. It is held in mid-September when Unity members all over the world gather in their own congregations to participate. During this day of prayer, the names of all the people who have called or written in are silently read and remembered in prayer. This is a powerful concept ripe with potential. Imagine if on just this one day each year, people everywhere, from every denomination, from every religious tradition, gathered to pray? Imagine the power of prayer truly unleashed upon our world.

All of us need to be touched in the deepest parts of our lives to have our spirit uncapped. If you uncap it, it will go everywhere. That's why we're here.

—*Reverend Cecil Williams*

I have a friend who came from a very poor family. One year, her parents told her they had no money to celebrate Christmas. She was heartbroken, but there wasn't anything to be done. At Sunday School, she happened to mention it to a friend, who told her parents. When the girl and her family were at church the Sunday before Christmas, a group of Sunday School parents snuck into her house, put up a tree and surrounded it with presents, and stocked the refrigerator with food. When the family opened the door, they were stunned and thrilled to see the surprise. Needless to say, it was their best Christmas ever!

You give but little when you give of your possessions. It is when you give of yourself that you truly give.

—*Kahlil Gibran*

I am a mother of three children (ages fourteen, twelve, and three) and have recently completed my college degree. The very last class I took was a sociology course taught by a truly inspiring instructor. Her last assignment was called "Smile." We were asked to go out and smile at three people and document their reactions. Since I am a very friendly person and love to smile at everyone, I thought this would be a piece of cake.

Soon after I was given the assignment my husband, youngest son, and I went out to McDonald's. It was a cold, crisp March morning and while standing in line waiting to be served, I noticed everyone in the line—including my husband—slowly backing away. An overwhelming sense of panic was coming over me as I turned to see why they had moved. The first thing I noticed was a horrible body odor and then I saw, standing behind me, two obviously very unfortunate men.

As I looked down at the short gentleman close to me, he was smiling. His beautiful sky-blue eyes were full of God's light. He said, "Good day," as he counted the few coins he had been clutching. The second man fumbled with his hands as he stood behind his friend. I realized the second man was mentally deficient and the blue-eyed gentleman was his salvation.

I held my tears as I stood there with them. The young lady at the counter asked them what they wanted. He said, "Coffee is all, Miss," because that was all they could afford to buy to be able to sit in the restaurant to warm up. I felt a strong compulsion to reach out and embrace the man with blue eyes, and that was when I noticed all the eyes in the restaurant upon me. I smiled and asked the lady behind the counter to give me two extra breakfast meals on a separate tray. I then walked around the corner to the table they had chosen, put the tray on the table and laid my hand on his cold hand. He looked up at me, with tears in his eyes and said, "Thank you." I leaned over and said, "I did not do this for you. . . . God is here working through me to give you hope."

I started to cry as I walked away to join my husband and son. When I sat down my husband smiled at me and said, "That is why God gave you to me, to give me hope." We held hands for a moment, and at that time we knew that only because of the Grace that we had been given were we able to give. We are not churchgoers, but we are believers. That day showed me the pure light of God's sweet love.

Everyone can be great because everyone can serve.

—Dr. Martin Luther King, Jr.

I live in a low-income apartment complex. Many of my neighbors are single mothers struggling to get by, and sometimes you can feel despair almost all around you. It is just so difficult to raise kids, hold down a job, and try to make something better of your life at the same time.

But there is one man who lives here who I swear must have been given to us by God. He is both physically and mentally handicapped, but has managed to take care of himself by working part-time at a fast-food place and collecting cans and bottles to recycle. He knows us all by name and greets us all when we leave each morning and return each evening. He's always there to help out, although we are all careful not to take advantage of him. He loves kids, and there isn't a day when at least one of the kids from the apartments can't be spotted hanging around the playground with him, being pushed on the swing or playing in the sandbox. When you need to rush out to the store, he is always willing to keep an eye on the kids for awhile. But mostly, he is just always there, always smiling, reminding us that we are more than the sum of all our problems.

Laughter dulls the sharpest pain and flattens out the greatest stress. To share it is to give a gift of health.

—*Barbara Johnson*

I have lived in a retirement home for five years. I'm old, can barely get around any more, but I still have most of my faculties about me. Every Christmas the ladies from a local church group show up to "brighten" our holiday. Trouble is, for most of them it just doesn't go off too well. They are all smiles and pleasantness, but it's obvious that it's all a performance. I think seeing so many elderly people scares the daylights out of them—and that just stretches their smiles even more.

But last year I got a real treat. One of the ladies had dragged along her son, and while the women were all fussing around, he came up to me and said, "How'd you ever get so old?" His mom was embarrassed as could be, but I just burst out laughing. I told him I didn't know how it had happened; I just kept on living. Then I told his mom to leave him with me for awhile to keep me company. I had more fun talking to that boy than I've had in years. He was just a pure, honest kid who was willing to talk to a wrinkled-up old man.

Kindness. Don't leave home without it.

—*Ng Hei-Di*

I'm in fifth grade. One day my mom was working on typing up something for her business and I heard her say to herself, "There's so much to do." I saw the dishes needed to be done and vacuuming too. So I just started doing the chores. When she saw this, my mom was happy. I felt good by doing something nice.

Whoever receives one little child like this in My name receives Me.

—*Matthew 18:5*

Twenty-five years ago, I was a young, single mother with an eighteen-month-old son who suffered from chronic respiratory infections. Many a night was spent in the emergency room of the local hospital.

We had set out one afternoon to visit a friend when I noticed my son tugging at his right ear. Glancing at the back mirror, I could see that his eyes had already taken on that glassy look that was a sure sign of the fever to follow. I was more than a little nervous, because I wasn't sure how much further it was to my friend's house and I knew nothing of the area.

After a few more miles had passed, I saw that my son was having a convulsion on the back seat! This had never happened before and I panicked. Yanking the car to the side of the road, I managed to grab him and hoist him over the seat to me. By this time he had stopped convulsing but was unconscious. His face was flushed, but his lips were drained of all color. I could feel the fear set in as I frantically looked for anyone or anything to help us. Unbelievably, the entrance to a hospital lay directly across the street.

The emergency room was packed as we blasted through the door. People were scattered around the room like discarded trash, barely moving as I made my way through. I stumbled to the nurse, placing my son on the counter. He was still unconscious, with a slight foam at his lips. The nurse shot us a cursory glance and back to her papers she went. Somehow I found my voice to beg her to look at my son. The first words out of her mouth were to ask whether I had $20 to pay for the services.

I didn't have any money on me. I don't think I ever felt so small or alone before or since. My son was going to die because I didn't have $20! I pleaded with her to get a doctor and promised to pay. In return, she gave me directions to the community hospital fifteen miles across a town I had never been in.

I turned and headed for the door, my son in my arms. Then, out of the crowd a very plain woman walked to the desk and lay down $20 on the counter. Softly she said, "Maybe now this baby can get some medical care?" I stood rooted to the spot, afraid there would be another hurdle to cross. When I turned to thank this savior of a woman, she was gone.

I don't know the name of my angel and I'm sure it doesn't matter. What does matter is that this woman came forward and delivered a random act of kindness that not only saved my son's life but restored my belief in humankind.

Let brotherly love continue. Do not forget to entertain strangers, for by so doing some have unwittingly entertained angels.

—Hebrews 13:1–2

I live in southern Alabama, and one summer we got word a hurricane was coming our way. We waited as long as we could, but when it became clear it was heading straight for us, we packed up the whole extended family in five cars and headed north on Interstate 65. We were looking for a storm shelter but hadn't found one by the time we reached Montgomery. Not knowing what to do, we went to a local church where a very nice woman contacted the Red Cross for us, only to find out there were no shelters available.

We had nowhere to go and couldn't afford to put the whole group of us up in a motel. Just as we were worrying about our situation the woman at the church said, "You know. . . . We just bought a house but we haven't moved in yet, why don't you all stay there?" We couldn't believe the offer. We thought she was going way above and beyond to let us stay in her new home, but that wasn't all. She had the power and water turned on for us, she brought furniture, and the neighbors brought food. We stayed for three nights until the hurricane danger had passed, using their power and water and their new home, and she wouldn't even think about accepting any money. We will always be grateful for the help she gave to total strangers in a tough time.

True Christianity is love in action.

—David O. McKay

A high school girl I know never got along with her father, and after her mother died, things got worse and worse. One day, during a particularly bad fight, her father kicked her out of the house. A neighbor brought her to school and explained to the principal why she was late. Upon hearing the story, the principal promptly offered to take her in. With the help of the principal and his family, the girl survived it all. She is now nineteen and married, with a two-and-a-half-month-old baby.

Our most valuable possessions are those which can be shared without lessening: those which, when shared, multiply.

—*William H. Danforth*

Late one evening my boyfriend and I were walking the four blocks from my house to his. As we walked, we noticed a woman about half a block ahead who looked like she'd fallen off her bike and was crying on the grass. We immediately ran over to her.

By the huddled position she was in, I thought she might be hurt and asked her if she was. "No," she sniffled, "I'm just sort of having an emotional breakdown." My boyfriend, who is not comfortable with conflict, walked on ahead. I was tempted to go too, but then I looked back at her. She looked so scared and alone. I put my hand on her shoulder and asked her softly, "Do you need a hug?"

She smiled so brightly it made her tears sparkle. She got up. I held her in my arms and let her cry some more. Then she stopped crying. "You're a very special person. No matter what happened, you deserve to be treated lovingly," I whispered as she began to pull away. "Thank you so much," she laughed. "You're an angel and you made me feel like one too."

I told her to do something good for herself that night, and she got back on her bike and rode away, waving.

ACKNOWLEDGMENTS

Many of the stories in this book came from letters and e-mail messages to the Random Acts of Kindness Foundation. A garland of thanks to all of those around the world who shared stories and otherwise made this book possible:

Suzanne Albertson; Alicia Alvrez; June Andrew; Ame Beanland; Ross Bolf; Chua Guat Mei; Cate Daniell; Bernadette Debbs; Robin Demers; Sharon Donovan; Nicole Drumheller; Lori Dunham; Carole Elliott; Will and Shelly Glennon; Melissa Fumia; Kyle Gray; Paula Hardin; the children of Harrison Elementary in Lakewood, Ohio; Martha Hills McVay; Tom King; Brenda Knight; Amelia Kridler; Nina Lesowitz; Lim Hsin Mei; Everton Lopez; Annette Madden; Violet Blaha Manteufel; Nancy Margolis; the children of Mary Hanley Catholic School in Edmonton, Canada; Donald, Steve, Louise, and Beth McIlraith; Maria McCormick; Kim Mitchell; Kara-Lynn Murphy; Anna Murray; Ng Hei-Dei; Sky Parker; David Pettitt; Pamela Polland; Phyllis Rowberry; Mary Jane Ryan; Sherai St. Claire; Claudia Schaab; members of the Singapore Kindness Movement; Claudia Smelser; Leslie Smith; Brenda Rae Souza; Barbara Bellamy Stoker; Tang Tuck Wing; Ryan Tassey; Jim Tran; Kari Watkins; Sandi Wilson; Jeffery Wood.

The Random Acts of Kindness™ Foundation

The Random Acts of Kindness™ Foundation is a nonprofit organization supporting tens of thousands of people who are committed to spreading kindness throughout the world. Formed in 1995, it currently organizes National Random Acts of Kindness™ Week, a year-round "Kindness in the Schools" project, a wellness program for businesses and organizations, and it serves as a founding committee member of the World Kindness Movement.

Every year since its debut, the Random Acts of Kindness™ Week celebration has nearly doubled in size: more than 450 communities, cities, and counties and thousands of schools, hospitals, churches, libraries, youth organizations, and bookstores in the United States and abroad participated in 1999.

To learn more about Random Acts of Kindness™ and to become part of a global network of people devoted to promoting kindness throughout the world, please call 800-660-2811, e-mail **info@actsofkindness.org,** or contact us online at **www.actsofkindness.org.**

Habitat for Humanity International

Founded in 1976 by Millard Fuller and his wife Linda, Habitat for Humanity International is a nonprofit, ecumenical Christian housing ministry that seeks to eliminate poverty housing and homelessness from the world by inviting people from all walks of life to work together in partnership to help build houses with families in need. Habitat has built more than 70,000 houses around the world, providing some 350,000 people in more than 2,000 communities with safe, decent, affordable shelter. For more information or to volunteer in your community, contact your local affiliate or the Habitat headquarters:

Habitat for Humanity
121 Habitat Street
Americus, GA 31709-3498

(800) 422-4828 (U.S.) or (912) 924-6935
e-mail: info@habitat.org
Web site: www.habitat.org